AIRCRAFT OF RED FLAG
THE ULTIMATE AIR-TO-AIR COMBAT EXERCISE

SCOTT CUONG TRAN AND NICK TRAN

KEY Books

Dedication
For Jane Tran

Published by Key Books
An imprint of Key Publishing Ltd
PO Box 100
Stamford
Lincs
PE19 1XQ

www.keypublishing.com

The right of Scott Cuong Tran and Nick Tran to be identified as the authors
of this book has been asserted in accordance with the Copyright, Designs and
Patents Act 1988 Sections 77 and 78.

Copyright © Scott Cuong Tran and Nick Tran, 2020

ISBN 978 1 913870 11 9

Typeset by SJmagic DESIGN SERVICES, India.

FRONT COVER IMAGE: An F-16C Fighting Falcon of the 65th Aggressor Squadron banks after take-off for a Red Flag mission as part of the Red Force.

TITLE PAGE IMAGE: A B-52 Stratofortress from Barksdale AFB lands after a tough Red Flag mission on the Nevada Test and Training Range.

CONTENTS PAGE IMAGE: A pair of A-10C Warthogs head out on a Red Flag strike mission. These fearsome aircraft can loiter for hours with large payloads, endearing them to troops on the ground.

CONTENTS

The sign at the entrance to Nellis Air Force Base makes it clear who owns the base and the skies above Nevada.

INTRODUCTION

The United States Air Force (USAF) provides training to make sure pilots and their very expensive aircraft can survive the harsh realities of combat. The USAF believes that surviving a minimum of ten combat missions gives adequate experience to perform at a high level in real-world situations. In order to provide a relatively safe and controlled environment to replicate these first ten missions, the USAF created the Red Flag exercises in 1975.[1] Since then, Red Flag has evolved into one of the largest air combat training exercises in the world, attracting participants from all corners of the globe.

Red Flag has its origins in the Vietnam War, as the USAF looked to increase its air-to-air kill ratios with dissimilar air combat training (DACT) for its pilots. For instance, Vietnam-era training pitted F-4 Phantoms against other F-4 Phantoms in air-to-air combat, yet their opponents did not fly Phantoms, so this aerial sparring practice was not as practical as it could have been. To address this insufficiency, several training programs were implemented to provide DACT, including the 4477th Test and Evaluation Squadron known as the Red Eagles. The Red Eagles were able to procure actual Soviet-built aircraft and demonstrate their performance to American fighter pilots.[2] Similarly, Red Flag supplies an "Aggressor" squadron as the "Red Force" opponents to test and train the "Blue Force" friendly aircraft. The Aggressors, under the 57th Wing, use tactics and flight characteristics specific to potential adversaries against the Blue Force to help them gain valuable experience.

Red Flag also helps the Air Force on the front line, because experienced aviators can contribute on the first day they arrive on the battlefield, as opposed to rookie pilots who would need to be broken in when they initially arrive in the combat zone. Typically, a new pilot would fly several "milk-run" missions to get their feet wet, but this took them and their instructors away from the actual fighting. Some estimates suggest that there would be a 30 percent increase in aircraft available to theater commanders if pilots were ready for action on day one.[3] Prior to Red Flag, the attitude toward combat training was simply that it was too difficult to replicate and therefore no attempt was made to provide relevant combat scenarios. However, Red Flag proved to not only the USAF, but also to all branches of the American military, that realistic training was possible, resulting in new exercises including the US Navy's Strike University, which coordinated with the famous Top Gun for a total force exercise.[4] The creation of Red Flag had a profound effect on the way militaries instruct their soldiers, as it allowed them to be as close to combat as possible without going to war.

Red Flag provides a number of unique scenarios for their visitors. Specifically, the missions can include defensive counterair (protect a position), offensive counterair (gain access to an area), dynamic targeting (neutralize strategic sites), counterland (close air support), irregular warfare (special operations), and space and cyberspace operations. Also, Red Flag pilots get to hone their basic fighter maneuvers (BFM) and air combat maneuvers (ACM); however, this exercise is not the place for beginner aviators. Students are expected to already be proficient with their aircraft and to be able to integrate their knowledge and expertise into a large air operation. Being able to win a one-versus-one engagement is not the goal of Red Flag, but rather it is to win an entire campaign. The results of Red Flag speak for themselves: since its inception, only one US aircraft has been lost to air-to-air combat.

Because of the USAF's many successes, most pilots have never operated in a contested environment, making Red Flag instruction even more crucial. The American public has taken air superiority for granted, and airmen must take precautions to ensure they do not become complacent. In order to prevent the USAF from losing its edge on the battlefield, Red Flag participants must take their schooling seriously. Maintaining control of the skies against a near-peer adversary requires the Red Flag exercises to be as rigorous and difficult as possible. Red Flag also allows visitors a chance to visit the Threat Training Facility, affectionately known as the "Petting Zoo." Here, the 547th Intelligence Squadron has assembled dozens of examples of possible enemy aircraft, surface-to-air-missiles (SAMs), anti-aircraft artillery, and armor that allied countries may face in the field. Those who partake in Red Flag get to touch and feel the tools used by their adversaries, giving them a better understanding of their battlespace.

However, Red Flag is not exclusively about air combat. Current Red Flag exercises are designed to simulate an expeditionary deployment, meaning all aspects of a combat scenario are simulated as closely as possible, including maintenance, logistics, interdiction, and search and rescue. This provides realistic training not only for the pilots, but also for the personnel performing maintenance, planning, security, and other support functions. As a result, all members of a squadron are ready to deploy and perform at a high level after Red Flag. During a normal fiscal year, at least three Red Flag exercises are conducted.

Nellis Air Force Base (AFB), located in fabulous Las Vegas, Nevada, is home to the Red Flag exercises and the Aggressor squadrons. Training occurs on the Nevada Test and Training Range (NTTR), which provides nearly 5,000 square miles of restricted military airspace and 12,000 square miles of total training area.[5] Some units at Nellis AFB include the USAF Warfare Center, 57th Wing, 99th Air Base Wing, and 926th Wing. Nellis AFB hosts international allied units for Red Flag in order to promote joint operations and international cooperation among the United States and her allies. Since 1975, 29 countries have participated with the US along with several observer nations.[6]

Red Flag is not only important for military air forces, but it is also a boon to aviation photographers. International tour groups bring photographers from abroad to Nellis AFB so that they can take pictures of aircraft taking off and landing. Most photographers stay outside the gate and chase the planes around as they fly in Red Flag, while a lucky few are invited inside for a closer look. Photographers will sometimes listen to the air traffic control tower on portable radio scanners to get to a more advantageous position. The airmen on base surely get a chuckle as they watch a gaggle of photographers try to run (hobble in most cases) into good spots while toting heavy and expensive camera equipment. As with the military units participating in Red Flag, a sense of camaraderie exists between those who are willing to sit in the sweltering Vegas heat to take pictures of airplanes. This book showcases some of the amazing aircraft that participate in Red Flag and provides pictorial documentation. These images were taken during Red Flag 2018 through 2020.

PHOTOGRAPHING RED FLAG

Nellis AFB is situated in the northeastern portion of Las Vegas and is easily accessible for photographs to be taken from the north and south, which makes it perfectly situated for snapping pictures during take-off and landing. The air base itself has two runways, labelled 03L/R and 21L/R, which run parallel to each other. A lucky photographer will get to see three take-offs per day: one in the morning, one at approximately 1200 hours, and a night launch at 2000 hours. A typical sortie lasts about two hours, so it will not take long to photograph the recovery.

The most popular spot to photograph Red Flag, especially when the aircraft are performing "FLEX" departures, is the Las Vegas Motor Speedway, which is north of Nellis AFB. A FLEX departure is where an aircraft takes off and banks toward a waypoint north of Nellis AFB, known as FLEX, providing an excellent topside view. Photographers park their vehicles along Las Vegas Boulevard at the intersections of Checkered Flag Lane and Speedway Boulevard and set up their equipment on the side of the road. Las Vegas Motor Speedway is the best place to photograph midday and afternoon flights as the lighting is perfect, whereas the morning sun will backlight the aircraft.

Photographers may also camp out further south along Las Vegas Boulevard to capture the base and get a closer look at the runway. However, some areas along the fence are too close for comfort for USAF Security Forces, and they have been known to chase people away. It is paramount to follow all instructions from military personnel and respect their boundaries as, after all, watching the aircraft of Red Flag is an incredible privilege.

Due south of the base are residential areas that provide the best spots for photographing morning flights. Many photographers line up along East Cheyenne Avenue to snap pictures of recoveries. Depending on the approach angle, it is possible to capture the nearby mountains behind the landing aircraft, which give a unique backdrop for aviation photography.

Each photographer has their preferred equipment and cameras, and most of the images in this book were taken with a Canon 1DX Mk II. It is recommended to have at least a 200mm lens, which is sufficient along East Cheyenne Avenue as the approaching planes are relatively close. At Las Vegas Motor Speedway, a 600mm lens is suggested, since the flight paths can push the aircraft further away from Las Vegas Boulevard. Because of the size of the lenses, many photographers bring tripods or monopods to provide stability and compensate for the massive weight of the equipment. Some have action cameras mounted on their heads so they can take videos while snapping pictures at the same time, which allows them to also capture the incredible roar of the jet engines.

There are usually a few photographers at each spot, each with their own favorite areas and angles. Many people come to simply watch the exercise and observe the might of the USAF and its allies. Some spectators are military veterans who share stories about their experiences at Red Flag, providing excellent real-time commentary. The most important takeaway is to have fun, enjoy the beauty of flight, and participate in the aviation community. Although each location offers its own advantages and disadvantages, there is no bad place to observe and capture the Flag!

CHAPTER 1
SUPPORT AIRCRAFT

The axiom "an army marches on its stomach" is as applicable today as it was since the beginning of warfare. A pilot cannot fly if he is hungry or does not have the proper uniform and equipment. No matter how fast, technologically advanced, stealthy, or sleek a fighter aircraft is, it cannot take off without fuel and cannot fight the enemy if the pilot does not know where to go. Support and logistics are the backbone of any successful military. Good commanders understand the importance of properly supplying their troops, and today they rely on heavy lift and transport aircraft to keep their troops in the fight.

The airmen who maintain and operate these aircraft are the unsung heroes of the Air Force. They often do not get the recognition they deserve for their work, but without them, the USAF cannot "Fly, Fight, and Win." Some of the important missions of these support aircraft include reconnaissance and intelligence gathering, command and control, transport, refueling, and search and rescue. These aircraft perform missions that heavily integrate with front-line aircraft, often going into harm's way. For instance, air refueling tankers flew well within the range of Iraqi surface-to-air missiles in *Desert Storm*, with a projected ten percent casualty rate. Fortunately, the tankers were able to complete their missions without any losses, but the threat was very real and imminent.[7]

Although there are no major Hollywood movies about tankers, transport, or intelligence, surveillance, target acquisition, and reconnaissance (ISTAR) aircraft, the spirit of the Duke of Marlborough, who revolutionized military logistics in the 17th and 18th centuries,[8] flies with these dedicated airmen. These aircraft are often the first to take off from Nellis AFB in order to scope out the battlefield and provide intelligence for the fighters and bombers during Red Flag exercises. Helicopter rescue squadrons arrive on station before the fighters take off and stand by ready to recover any downed pilots. This chapter hopes to bring light to some of these behind-the-scenes aircraft and highlight the importance of good supply lines and reconnaissance.

Because of their unsung nature, the support aircraft are not as well known as the fighters. However, the Red Flag support aircraft provide excellent photo opportunities because of their size and unhurried flight path: it is impossible to miss the massive C-17 flying overhead, and its reduced landing speed gives plenty of time and subject matter to waiting photographers. In short, the tankers, transports, intelligence, and command and control aircraft are a hidden gem at Red Flag.

OPPOSITE: An EC-130H Compass Call takes off to perform an electronic countermeasures mission.

A Boeing E-3B Sentry based out of Tinker AFB in Oklahoma lands at Nellis AFB. It is an Airborne Warning and Control System (AWACS) aircraft, and its mission is to detect targets in the air and on the ground and relay that information to the Air Battle Manager (ABM) who directs and controls aircraft in the battlespace.

The Sentry is based on the civilian Boeing 707/320 airframe and is heavily modified for military purposes, most notably with the large rotating radar dome mounted on top of the aircraft, which has a range in excess of 250 miles.

This Sentry, serial number 73-1675, is part of the 552d Air Control Wing at Tinker AFB, Oklahoma. Its crew varies in number from 13 to 19 depending on its mission profile.

NATO also operates 14 E-3s, and Red Flag helps train both US and NATO crews, allowing coalition members to work together and understand the finer points of air command and control.

OPPOSITE: Another important aircraft that helps manage battles is the Boeing E-8C Joint Surveillance Target Attack Radar System (Joint STARS). It is based on the Boeing 707/300 airframe and modified with radar and communications systems to provide ground intelligence for Air Force, Army, and Marine Corps commanders.

ABOVE: As seen on the forward belly of the Joint STARS, the downward-looking radar identifies land targets and has a range of over 150 miles.

LEFT: This E-8C is from Robins AFB in Georgia, serial number 01-2005. It carries up to 22 crew members from both the Air Force and Army depending on its mission.

OPPOSITE: At the end of a Red Flag mission, this Joint STARS comes in for a landing at Nellis AFB.

No one Kicks Ass Without Tanker Gas! This is the motto of the aerial refueling tankers, abbreviated to NKAWTG, and explains the importance of their mission, which is to ensure aircraft have enough gas to get to and from their targets. This tanker example, serial number 63-8885, is a KC-135R Stratotanker and is part of the 92d Air Refueling Wing (active component) as well as the 141st Air Refueling Wing (reserve component) from Fairchild AFB in Spokane, Washington.

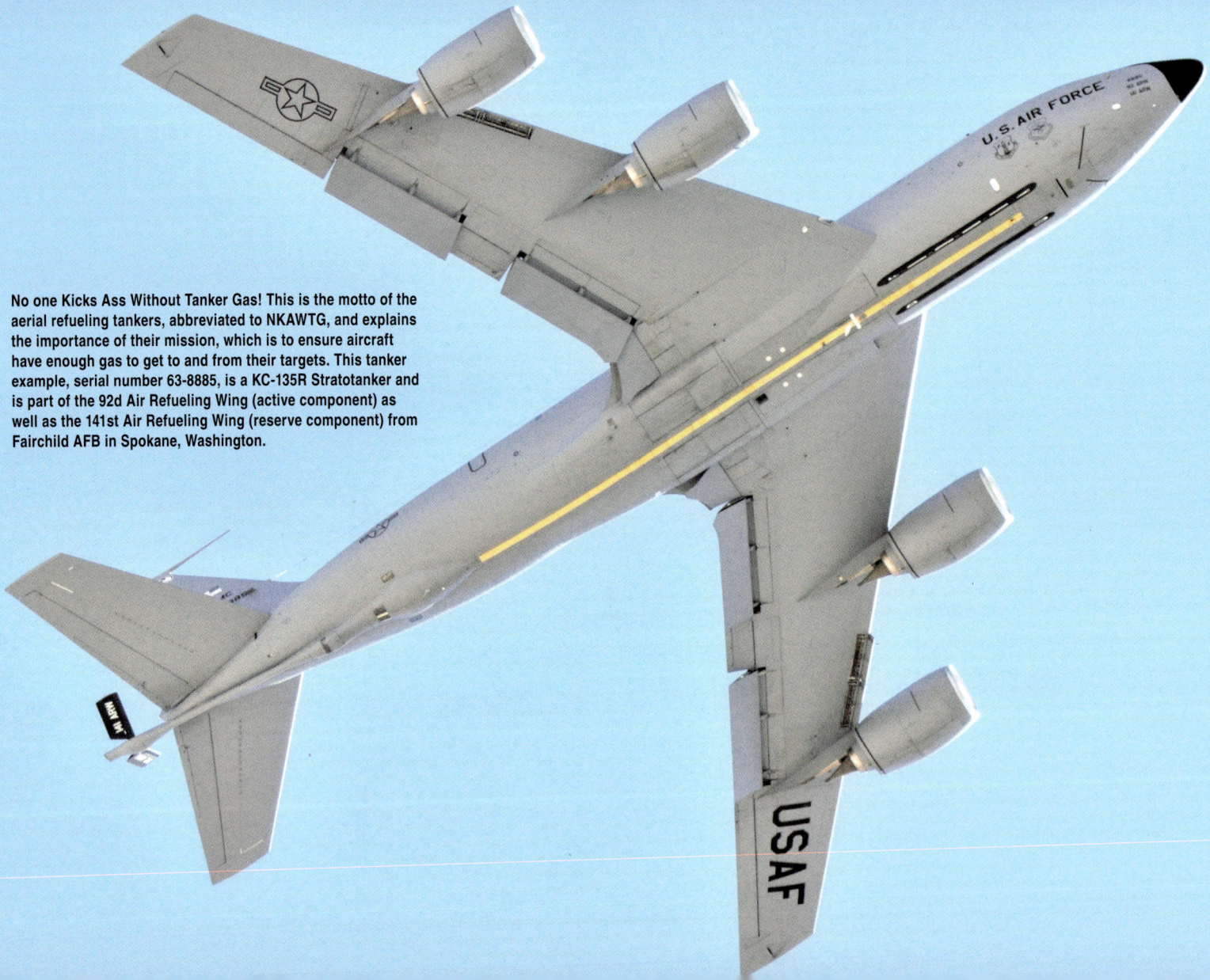

Another KC-135R, serial number 64-14837, hails from the 927th Air Refueling Wing in MacDill AFB near Tampa, Florida. The KC-135R has three crew members, including one boom operator. The boom operator controls the refueling boom at the aft of the aircraft in order to connect it to a thirsty customer. The Stratotanker can offload up to 83,000lb of fuel.

One of the air refueling hubs is at McConnell AFB in Wichita, Kansas, and provides a home to the KC-135Rs of the 22d Air Refueling Wing (active component) and the 931st Air Refueling Wing (reserve command). This aircraft is serial number 60-0356.

Another McConnell Stratotanker, serial number 58-0065, comes in for a touch-and-go landing after feeding hungry fighters. The boom operator window can be seen at the base of the refueling boom. The boom operator looks out of this window and gives instructions to the recipient pilot.

The yellow stripe on the belly of the KC-135R is to help the refueling pilot align with the tanker. Additionally, a series of lights are used to provide fueling status: green for fuel flow, amber for inhibited flow, and red for a breakaway command.

A unique mission at Red Flag is performed by this Lockheed EC-130H Compass Call, serial number 73-1586, belonging to the 55th Electronic Combat Group from Davis-Monthan AFB in Arizona. The Compass Call disrupts enemy communications via jamming or other types of offensive electronic attack measures. The EC-130H participates in Suppression of Enemy Air Defenses (SEAD) by blinding, or otherwise negating, enemy ground-based radars.

One of the more dangerous and essential missions in the Air Force is Search and Rescue (SAR). At Red Flag, this HC-130J Combat King II, serial number 10-0717, is from the 23d Wing, which can trace its heritage back to the famous Flying Tigers who fought in China in the Second World War.

The Combat King II can perform recovery operations day or night in contested conditions and is appreciated by all pilots who fly into a combat zone.

No territory can be held without troops on the ground. The Army provides a contingent of their soldiers and aircraft to work with the various air forces at Red Flag. Here, an Army Black Hawk helicopter launches from Nellis AFB in support of simulated ground missions.

The Pave Hawk's primary mission is combat rescue, which includes downed pilots and injured soldiers. The HH-60G transports the vaunted Pararescue Jumpers (PJs), an elite Air Force unit whose sole mission is to go behind enemy lines and rescue friendly personnel.

ABOVE: Not to be outdone by the Army, the Air Force also provides helicopters to train at Red Flag. This Sikorsky HH-60G Pave Hawk, serial number 91-26352, is a rescue helicopter from the 66th Rescue Squadron at Nellis AFB.

RIGHT: Although they do not fly, maintenance personnel are extremely important to the Air Force mission and deserve mention in this logistics and support chapter. This view through the fence shows the tarmac full of aircraft that are being serviced by dedicated airmen. Aircraft would stay grounded without the professional dedication of maintainers who must suffer while working in the harsh Nevada environment.

CHAPTER 2
STRATEGIC INTERDICTION

An important aspect of warfare is the strategic interdiction of crucial enemy facilities. This entails disabling key command and control centers, communications hubs, and manufacturing plants. The objective is to take away the enemy's means to continue their fight. Heavy and long-range aircraft are required for these missions and represent an integral part of an air campaign. Red Flag seeks to incorporate those missions and aircraft by inviting heavy bombers from the Air Force Global Strike Command (AFGSC). These bombers are often escorted by Blue Force aircraft, which protect them from the Red Force fighters. Additionally, the bombers practice their aerial refueling skills with the support aircraft shown in the previous chapter.

Red Flag allows the bombers to train in an unfamiliar and contested environment. If a bomber crew simply follows a flight plan, drops their payload on time, and goes home without drama, they have not learned as much about themselves, their aircraft, and their tactics as they could have if challenges had been thrown at them during their mission. During Red Flag missions, crews must learn how to avoid threats, coordinate with friendly escorts, and defend themselves. Although a B-52 might seem rather helpless in a combat zone, the electronic warfare officer (EWO) is ready to jam or otherwise obfuscate enemy radars to prevent missile shots so Red Flag provides simulated threats for the EWO to counter, such as an S-400 Triumph (SA-21 Growler) system.[9]

Bombers fly some of the most dangerous combat missions. They are especially vulnerable because of their slow speed and large radar cross section and are a high-priority target for the enemy because of their destructive power. For instance, during Operation *Linebacker II* in December 1972, 15 B-52 Stratofortresses and crew were lost, which was two percent of the total sorties. Yet their effect was tremendous, as the North Vietnamese were forced to the negotiating table after 15,000 tons of ordnance was dropped in just 11 days, crippling the power grid, oil supplies, and imports.[10] During *Linebacker II*, the Stratofortresses were assisted by a myriad of other aircraft, including tankers, electronic attack aircraft, and fighter escorts, demonstrating the importance of teamwork and interoperability, highlighting the necessity of Red Flag exercises.

Although the roar of the engines from the fighter aircraft can be deafening, the powerplants of the B-1 and B-52 provide their own unique contributions to the cacophony that is Red Flag. The rumbling of B-1 engines on take-off can seemingly be felt throughout the entirety of Las Vegas, and the smoke belching from the Pratt and Whitney turbofans of the B-52 makes the smoggiest Los Angeles day seem clear in comparison. The photographers of Red Flag are without a doubt aware when a strategic bomber is leaving Nellis AFB for a mission!

OPPOSITE: This B-1B zooms up from take-off for a mission. Notably, this Lancer has nose art commemorating the members of the Second World War Doolittle Raid with a "Ruptured Duck" insignia closest to the cockpit.

The B-1B is part of Global Strike Command. This example, serial number 86-0118, is from the 37th Bomb Squadron from Ellsworth AFB in Rapid City, South Dakota. The Sniper Advanced Targeting Pod, designated as the AN/AAQ-33, is hung behind the front landing gear and provides targeting information for air-to-ground weapons.

OPPOSITE: Bad to the Bone! The Boeing (formerly Rockwell) B-1B Lancer is a swing-wing heavy bomber designed for high-speed nuclear strikes during the Cold War. Although no longer nuclear-capable, the Lancer is still able to carry a 75,000lb conventional payload. The Lancer gets its nickname from its numerical designation (B-One).

The small canards at the front of the Lancer are used to reduce buffeting during high-speed flight. This provides stability and reduces stress on the aircraft.

The Lancer carries all of its weapons internally to reduce its radar cross section, making it more difficult to find on radar.

As part of Operation *Enduring Freedom* in Afghanistan, B-1Bs dropped over 40 percent of all bombs in the first six months of the conflict. Although conventional bombing was not its original mission, the Lancer was able to perform admirably in a combat environment.

This fantastic rear view of a Lancer taking off at sunset showcases the sleek lines and variable sweep wings.

ABOVE: A pair of B-1Bs from Ellsworth AFB head out on a Red Flag mission. Lancers are primarily based at Ellsworth AFB and Dyess AFB in Texas and have a test and evaluation group at Nellis AFB.

RIGHT: The Boeing B-52 Stratofortress has been the mainstay of the Air Force bomber corps since 1954 and is anticipated to remain in service until the 2050s. This variant is the B-52H and is part of the AFGSC. The Stratofortress has the appropriate nickname of "BUFF" which stands for Big Ugly Fat Fellow (some use a more colorful term).

This Stratofortress from Barksdale AFB, serial number 61-0012, is part of the 96th Bomb Squadron and is known as "Loko" according to its nose art, which is behind the cockpit.

Based at Minot AFB, this B-52H, serial number 60-0044, is a part of the 23d Bomb Squadron and is coming in for a landing after a Red Flag exercise.

Like the B-1B, "Loko" carries the Sniper Advanced Targeting Pod, as seen under the starboard wing.

This B-52H, serial number 60-0012, also hails from Minot AFB in North Dakota and is part of the 69th Bomb Squadron. The other B-52 base is at Barksdale AFB in Louisiana.

The Boeing F-15E Strike Eagle has increased payload and fuel capacities over the F-15C and is designed to provide close air support (CAS) for troops on the ground. This Strike Eagle, serial number 96-0200, is from the 422d Test and Evaluation Squadron.

CHAPTER 3
BLUE FORCE FIGHTERS

The Blue Force consists of the visiting units who come from all over the United States and the globe. They are as diverse as the geographic areas from which they hail and provide unique experiences that enhance their mission capabilities. The units must work together as a team to complete the missions assigned to them. They attack and defend targets at the Nevada Test and Training Range (NTTR), which include simulated convoys, airfields, bunkers, and surface-to-air missile sites. Although proud fighter pilots are focused on "winning" by defeating the Red Force aircraft, the main goal of Red Flag is for the Blue Force to learn to work as a team in a deployed environment and to get ready for a real-world situation.

As with any training, the Blue Force must start out slowly and increase the intensity of their exercises as the training progresses. Many of the units are working together for the first time and are required to understand their roles and responsibilities within the overall mission scope. Red Flag simulates the chaos involved in battle and many Blue Force veterans claim their Red Flag exercise was tougher than actual combat seen in *Desert Storm*, Operation *Enduring Freedom*, and Operation *Iraqi Freedom*.[11] The objective of Red Flag is to help young lieutenants and captains survive in the real world and participation with the Blue Force helps with that aim.

Although the exploits of fighter pilots have been well documented through innumerable books and movies, their importance and skill cannot be overstated. Because of the increased destruction bombers can bring, modern battlefields must be cleared of enemy aircraft so that ground operations do not incur unacceptable losses. The way to achieve air superiority is for pilots of fighter aircraft to be well trained in the art of air-to-air combat, which is why Red Flag is an essential part of every fighter pilot's curriculum. One fact the USAF is particularly proud of is that no member of the American military ground force has been killed due to enemy air attacks since the Korean War. One of the core principles of the USAF is to protect the boots on the ground, and fighters help keep those soldiers safe by clearing the skies of enemy bombers.

The Blue Force fighters at Red Flag provide much excitement for the photographers at Nellis AFB. They look to identify the different units of the visiting Blue Force and some will cheer for their hometown squadrons. Although involved in serious training, a few pilots will acknowledge the photographers on the ground by banking for better pictures after take-off and dipping their wings in salute.

A Boeing (formerly McDonnell-Douglas) F-15C Eagle from the 144th Fighter Wing based in Fresno, California, comes in for a landing to start Red Flag. This F-15C, serial number 86-0144, is part of the Air National Guard, showing that Red Flag is accessible to active, Guard, and reserve units.

LEFT: Another Eagle, serial number 82-0018, blasts its way to the Nevada Test and Training Range. The Eagle is part of the 422d Test and Evaluation Squadron at Nellis AFB, which is easily identified by the yellow and black checkers on the top of the tails and can trace its lineage back to the Second World War when the unit was a night fighting squadron. The 422d has a variety of aircraft, which it uses to experiment with new tactics and strategies.

BELOW: The Oregon Air National Guard is represented at Red Flag by this F-15C, serial number 84-0003, which is part of the 123d Fighter Squadron, known as the "Redhawks."

Another F-15C, serial number 82-0022, of the 422d Test and Evaluation Squadron, is seen here landing at Red Flag.

A pair of F-15Cs from the 422d Test and Evaluation Squadron is seen taking off at sunrise. Note that the lead F-15C, serial number 82-0022, is carrying a Talon HATE pod on its centerline pylon. This is used for battlefield communications between 4th and 5th generation aircraft.

Another Strike Eagle from the 422d offers this striking view of its engines as it lands at Red Flag. The Strike Eagle is affectionately known as the "Mudhen," in reference to its air-to-ground mission.

Two Mudhens soar over Nellis AFB on their way to another Red Flag exercise.

This Strike Eagle provides an excellent view of the various pods it carries for an air-to-ground mission. Underneath the port air intake is a Sniper Advanced Targeting Pod. The centerline station carries the AN/ASQ-236 "Dragon Eye" radar pod used for terrain mapping and intelligence gathering. The station below the starboard air intake is an AN/AAQ-13 Low Altitude Navigation and Targeting Infrared for Night (LANTIRN) that provides navigation and targeting information for the Mudhen, increasing its combat effectiveness, particularly at night.

BRRRT! That's the sound of freedom in the form of a 30mm cannon being fired from a Fairchild Republic A-10C Thunderbolt II, known as the "Warthog," in reference to its less-than-sleek appearance. The Warthog is an attack aircraft designed to provide close air support, and soldiers on the ground love its most famous weapon: the 30mm GAU-8/A seven-barrel Gatling gun.

The Warthog is designed to take serious punishment from surface-to-air weapons and the cockpit is so heavily armored, it is often referred to as a "titanium bathtub." There are many stories of an A-10C being heavily damaged by enemy fire but still being able to limp home and save the pilot.

This Warthog example, serial number 82-0658, is part of the 422d Test and Evaluation Squadron and is on its way to strike targets at Red Flag.

This fabulous four-ship formation of Warthogs makes its way to the Nevada Test and Training Range.

ABOVE: Although slated for retirement numerous times, the Warthog continues to defy the odds because of its incredible performance over the battlefield, where it can loiter for extended periods of time while carrying an impressive payload of up to 16,000lb.

LEFT: This A-10C shows off only a portion of its possible payload under its wings. In addition to its cannon, this aircraft carries a Sniper Advanced Targeting Pod, AGM-65 Maverick, and 2.75in Hydra rockets.

A "clean" Warthog, serial number 82-0665, takes off from Nellis AFB in support of Red Flag exercises and is part of the 422d.

A pair of Lockheed Martin F-16C Fighting Falcons, nicknamed "Vipers," make their way to a Red Flag mission.

This F-16C is carrying a full load that includes an AGM-88 High-speed Anti-Radiation Missile (HARM) which is used for Suppression of Enemy Air Defenses (SEAD) operations. It also carries a Sniper Advanced Targeting Pod and AN/ALQ-184 Electronic Counter Measures (ECM) pod.

The 77th Fighter Squadron from Shaw AFB in South Carolina sent this F-16C, serial number 94-0043, to participate in Red Flag. The speed brakes on either side of the engine are open for landing.

An exciting livery is shown on this F-16C, serial number 86-0336, commemorating the 70th anniversary of the 158th Fighter Wing and 134th Fighter Squadron. The tail depicts a Green Mountain Boy of the Burlington Air National Guard in Vermont.

Another member of the Green Mountain Boys, serial number 87-0312, lands after a Red Flag exercise.

This F-16C, serial number 88-0486, from Hill AFB in Utah is carrying an unusual payload that includes two Hydra rocket pods under its port wing. It is a combat veteran of Operation *Enduring Freedom* and is from the 4th Fighter Squadron, known as the "Fighting Fuujins."

Two heavily armed F-16Cs from the 77th Fighter Squadron "Gamblers" takes off for another Red Flag mission.

ABOVE: The tail art on this F-16C, serial number 92-3911, shows off its mission as a "Wild Weasel" aircraft, designed for SEAD operations. As a member of the 157th Fighter Squadron, it is part of the South Carolina Air National Guard.

LEFT: Another F-16 from the 157th Fighter Squadron comes in for a landing. The 157th are known as the "Swamp Foxes," so named after Brigadier General Francis Marion, who served in the Revolutionary War in South Carolina.

ABOVE: Red Devils at Red Flag! The Red Flag exercises also attract the attention of the United States Marine Corps F/A-18C Hornets of VMFA-232 based out of Marine Corps Air Station (MCAS) in Miramar.

BELOW LEFT: The Red Devils of VMFA-232 are the most decorated Marine Corps fighter squadron and can trace their lineage back to 1925. One of their most famous battles is the Second World War Battle of Guadalcanal, where they fought with the hodgepodge Cactus Air Force.

BELOW RIGHT: The Marines always bring exciting livery and this example, BuNo 165195, is no exception. The red tails are very distinguishable and reflect the squadron's motto: "The Devil Made Me Do It."

ABOVE: While the US Air Force uses F-16Cs for their SEAD missions, the US Navy uses the Boeing EA-18G Growler. Based on the F-18 Super Hornet airframe, the Growler uses AN/ALQ-218 detection pods on the wingtips and AN/ALQ-99 jamming pods on the pylons next to the fuel tanks to find and blind enemy radar. It has two crew members: a pilot and an electronic warfare officer.

LEFT: A three-ship formation of Red Devils heads out to the Nevada Test and Training Range to train with their Air Force brethren.

BELOW: US Navy aircraft are known for their fantastic paint jobs, and BuNo 168386 is no exception, with its tail showing off its mascot, a Yellow Jacket.

This Growler is from VAQ-131 "Lancers" and is flexing for the photographers on take-off.

Even the US Army gets involved in Red Flag. This Boeing AH-64E Apache helicopter takes off to provide support for simulated ground units.

This Apache is from the 1st Cavalry Division based out of Fort Hood, Texas. It is important for the Air Force to be able to coordinate with their Army counterparts, and Red Flag provides this opportunity.

This Lockheed Martin F-22 Raptor banks and flexes after take-off, giving photographers a wonderful topside view. The Raptor is the world's most advanced operational fighter and incorporates stealth, supercruise, and excellent maneuverability to provide air dominance over a battlespace.

ABOVE: Part of the maneuverability stems from the thrust-vectoring engines that can move up to 20 degrees to provide a deflected airflow.

RIGHT: To maintain its stealth features, the Raptor carries all its weapons internally, including its gun. This view shows the smooth belly of the Raptor as it comes in for a landing.

A pair of Raptors soars overhead at Nellis AFB as they hunt for targets. A portion of the Raptor's stealth capabilities comes from the radar-absorbing material and paint, which can cause some discoloration on the skin of the aircraft.

INSET: Another contributor to the Raptor's stealth is the angled shapes of the aircraft itself. The sharp edges of the Raptor have the same angles shown here, which are designed to reflect radar waves away from the receiver.

Two Raptors prepare to break for their Red Flag mission. They are part of the 422d, based at Nellis AFB.

This Lockheed Martin F-35A Lightning II, serial number 17-5237, banks after take-off and produces vapor trails from the wingtips. This occurs when the air pressure changes enough to force water vapor out of the air, creating a white and wispy trail. This example is from Hill AFB in Utah.

Like the F-22, the F-35A holds its weapons internally to preserve its stealth features. Additionally, the airframe is blended to prevent sharp angles as much as possible.

Sometimes, the pilots of Red Flag will acknowledge the photographers on the ground by showing off their aircraft. This F-35A, serial number 17-5271, opens its weapons bay doors for its admirers.

ABOVE: This F-35A, serial number 15-5130, from the 422d Test and Evaluation Squadron, lands after a Red Flag exercise.

RIGHT: If the Lightning II requires additional payloads for its mission, externally mounted pylons can be added. Although the pylons make the Lightning II less stealthy, they can be jettisoned after use.

CHAPTER 4
RED FORCE FIGHTERS

Red Force fighter pilots are among the best in the USAF. Their mission is to replicate the tactics and flight profiles of potential adversaries. In fact, many Red Force fighters are painted similarly to the type of aircraft they are meant to mimic, including the blue splinter camouflage used by the Su-27 Flanker. The Red Force is comprised of aircraft from the 64th Aggressor Squadron (64 AGRS), under the 57th Wing. The Aggressors fly 20 F-16C Fighting Falcons to provide realistic threats for the Blue Force to compete against. A professional and dedicated Aggressor force is necessary so that Blue Force units can focus on their own tactics and skills at their home base without the distractions of fully mastering the operations of their adversaries.

The Aggressors can trace their heritage to the Vietnam War and the need for the USAF to increase air-to-air kill ratios. The flying service recognized that pilots needed to practice against aircraft and pilots that they were unfamiliar with. For instance, an F-4 Phantom produces a distinct smoke pattern that can be easy to spot from a distance, whereas an opposing MiG-17 does not. Phantom pilots who fight against other Phantom pilots in training can pick up their opponents by looking for that smoke pattern, but in Vietnam, they were unable to find the exhaust trails from the MiG-17.[12] To rectify these deficiencies, the USAF created the Red Eagles (officially known as Constant Peg) and Aggressor programs to help pilots train against realistic threats. The Aggressors participate in all Red Flag exercises and are based at Nellis AFB. They without a doubt give their guests a run for their money by pushing them to their limits.

In addition to the Aggressors, Nellis AFB is home to the USAF Weapons School, which provides graduate-level instruction for airmen to become experts in their respective weapons and tactics. Although formerly known as Fighter Weapons School, the modern iteration has expanded its scope from just fighter tactics to include intelligence gathering, rescue operations, and even space and cyberspace integration. The Weapons School, along with the Aggressors and Red Flag, ensure that the USAF and its allies are well prepared to face threats in all aspects of the battlespace.

The Red Force F-16s are the highlight of the Red Flag experience due to the paint schemes and experience of the pilots. The liveries are unique and have been assigned antagonistic nicknames such as "Wraith," "Ghost," and "Shark." The Aggressors will acknowledge the photographers and sometimes even wave to ground observers. As a result, the pilots of the 64 AGRS have become fan favorites for photographers from around the world.

OPPOSITE: This stunning "Blue Splinter" F-16C Aggressor, serial number 86-0251, flexes after take-off.

This Aggressor F-16, serial number 84-0301, is painted in a "Blizzard" paint scheme, designed to mimic Cold War-era aircraft in Arctic camouflage.

Blizzard returns to Nellis AFB after a long day of chasing down Blue Force aircraft. The goal of the unique paint is to get Blue Force aircraft to get used to seeing schemes different from their own.

Not all Red Force aircraft have bright colors, but they still provide important training. This Aggressor is painted in the "Have Glass" low-visibility scheme, making it more difficult to find visually and on radar, as the paint has some radar-absorption capabilities.

An F-16C, serial number 90-0757, in normal US Air Force livery flies in support of Aggressor operations as part of the 57th Wing at Nellis AFB.

A spooky F-16C, serial number 86-0272, is painted dark gray with two bright red stars, known as "Shark," simulating paint schemes found on some Su-34 Fullbacks.

ABOVE: This Aggressor, serial number 86-0291, sports a "Desert Flanker" livery, a two-tone brown and tan scheme, similar to the Su-27 Flanker.

RIGHT: To simulate a MiG-23 Flogger, Aggressor, serial number 86-0299, has a "Lizard Scheme" utilizing green, brown, and tan colors.

The "Blue Flanker" Aggressor, serial number 84-0244, has three colors with two blues and one gray, a scheme widely used by the Su-27 Flanker.

Blue Splinter returns from a mission, possibly simulating the Su-27 Flanker, in both livery and performance.

A new paint scheme, known as "Ghost," has graced the airframes of the Aggressors and consists of blue digital camouflage.

Ghost was painted in 2019 as the result of an online poll and has been applied to F-16C serial number 84-0220.

This beautiful sunset could only be enhanced by Blue Splinter, Blizzard, Desert Flanker, and Blue Flanker flying in formation as they return to base.

Sometimes, Red Force aircraft play nice. Here, Blizzard flies with an EA-18 Growler, BuNo 166929 from VAQ-141.

Flying with the Aggressors is F-16C serial number 88-442, seen here flexing after take-off.

Sporting another fabulous Arctic paint scheme, this F-16C, serial number 86-0273, flies overhead with three colors: black, gray, and white.

An Arctic camouflaged ALCA banks after take-off. The ALCA was originally built in the Czech Republic and was designed for export sales.

CHAPTER 5
CONTRACT SUPPORT

An important aspect of dissimilar air combat training is to bring in contract aircraft to participate in Red Flag. One of the biggest contractors is Draken International, a regular operator at Red Flag. Draken operates a bevy of high-performance aircraft, including the L-159E Honey Badger, A-4 Skyhawk, and Mirage F1M, which have different flight characteristics from those of a Red Force F-16. Additionally, the contract adversaries help save the USAF money, as the L-159, A-4, and F1M are cheaper to operate and maintain, and every hour flown on a contract aircraft is one less flown on an Air Force jet, extending the life of front-line aircraft. Another benefit of hiring a private air force is that retired fighter pilots will still be able to train active military personnel by using their experience to contribute to the Red Force squadron. Debriefs are an integral part of the combat exercises, and Draken can provide accurate and useful information based on their previous military experience. Some other companies include ATAC, Top Air, Air USA, TacAir, Blue Air, and Top Aces.

Although a part of the Red Force and flying older and less capable aircraft, Draken pilots do not simply present themselves as cannon fodder. They are more than capable of defending themselves with their skills and technology, including advanced radar and electronic countermeasures. Draken pilots also have the advantage of focusing solely on flying without the sometimes-tedious administrative requirements found in the active Air Force. The Blue Force would be remiss to underestimate the professionals at Draken International.

Contractors have provided training support for the American military since its founding. In February 1778, Friedrich Wilhelm Ludolf Gerhard Augustin, better known as Baron von Steuben, arrived at Valley Forge in Pennsylvania to help General George Washington train his soldiers. Although ostensibly in the colonies to fight for the cause of independence, Baron von Steuben was primarily inspired by money and the chance to enhance his reputation as a military man. Whatever the motivation, he provided excellent training to the rebellious army and brought his experiences on the European battlefields with him, exaggerated as they were. His insights were able to turn a hodgepodge group of ragtag farmers into a precise and professional military force. The results of this contract training were tremendous, as the Continental Army was able to acquit themselves well at the Battle of Monmouth, standing tall in the face of repeated British musket attacks and bayonet charges.[13] Although contract military training tends to be overlooked, the lessons learned can be invaluable. Continuing the legacy of Baron von Steuben is Draken and their private air force at Red Flag.

Draken aircraft are easily identified by their unique liveries, often in digital form. Additionally, their logo is emblazoned on the side of the aircraft for easy identification (and advertisement!). Nellis photographers are eager to see the variety of aircraft that Draken operates, and because the company is constantly acquiring additional planes, it is always exciting to see who will show up for the Red Force.

A Douglas A-4K Skyhawk operated by Draken International takes off from Nellis AFB to support Red Air operations for Red Flag. This Skyhawk is a supersonic (Mach 1.3) fighter and, with upgrades performed in 2013, is a formidable foe.

This great side view of the Skyhawk shows off the Draken logo as well as the roundel of its former operator: the New Zealand Air Force.

An Arctic camouflage Skyhawk flies overhead after take-off. The Draken Skyhawks are fitted with advanced radars to lock on to the Blue Force aircraft, forcing them to take evasive action.

This Aero L-159E Honey Badger, known as an Advanced Light Combat Aircraft (ALCA), sports an awesome desert camouflage scheme.

Another ALCA comes in to land at Nellis AFB. It is a 4th generation fighter that provides excellent training opportunities to Blue Force opponents.

LEFT: This ALCA sports dummy sidewinder missiles and external fuel tanks to simulate an appropriate combat load during a Red Flag mission.

BELOW: Draken also operates the Dassault Mirage F1M high-performance fighter, which can reach speeds in excess of Mach 2. This F1M has a digital Arctic camouflage. Draken received most of its F1Ms as excess from the Spanish Air Force, which was looking to upgrade their fleet.

The ALCA can be equipped with a number of modern external pods, weapons, and countermeasures, challenging Blue Force pilots.

This British RAF F-35B Lightning II, ZM146/012, flexes on take-off. This Lightning II is from the famed 617 Squadron, the "Dambusters," based at RAF Marham.

CHAPTER 6

INTERNATIONAL PARTICIPANTS

While Red Flag is typically a US-centric exercise, many allied countries are invited in the name of international cooperation. Gone are the days of unilateral military actions, and the US Air Force recognizes the importance of bringing helpful participants into the fray. Per General James Mattis: "When you're going to a gunfight, bring all your friends with guns… and there is always room [on the battlefield] for those who want to be there alongside us."[14] The USAF aims to bring as many guns to the mix as possible at Red Flag. In addition to practicing together, these joint exercises allow different air forces to bounce ideas off each other to learn new tactics and strategies. Foreign units can also take the skills they have learned at Red Flag and bring them back to their home countries, making for well-trained allies around the world. Soft political power is another reason to include international air forces, as visitors can fully appreciate the capabilities of the USAF and hopefully see the value of having America as an ally. Since its inception, Red Flag has hosted 29 countries in addition to several countries observing the drills. Red Flag has also inspired other air exercises worldwide, such as Maple Flag held at CFB Cold Lake in Alberta, Canada, and Blue Flag, an Israeli-hosted biennial event.

The international guests of Red Flag use the exercise to practice their expeditionary abilities by deploying across oceans and bringing all the necessary personnel and equipment to an unfamiliar base. Working out logistical kinks is an added benefit to attending Red Flag. As an example, during Red Flag 20-1, five Royal Air Force (RAF) F-35Bs were scheduled to be refueled along the way to the United States but experienced tanker issues and were forced to land at a secondary airfield. Fortunately, the well-prepared RAF crews were able to execute their back-up plans to perfection and successfully made the trip across the Atlantic.[15] Participating in Red Flag has helped the RAF learn these valuable lessons in contingency planning.

For the photographers of Red Flag, it is always thrilling to see who will be participating in the exercises. Most of the photographers are American and relish the sight of new and foreign aircraft. At each Red Flag, there are a handful of international photographers who have made the trip to the United States and will celebrate when their home country's aircraft pass over. The spirit of global cooperation extends beyond the gates of Nellis AFB, as the photographers of all backgrounds share information with each other to get a better understanding of each other's air forces.

The Royal Air Force (RAF) has their airlift requirements met with the Boeing C-17 Globemaster III, and this example, ZZ174, made its way to Red Flag from RAF Brize Norton, representing 99 Squadron.

ABOVE: Typhoon ZK376 shows off its power by flexing out of Nellis AFB, giving an excellent view of its topside.

LEFT: The pride of the RAF fighter corps is the Eurofighter EF-2000 Typhoon FGR.4, represented here by ZK376 of 41 Squadron. A 4.5 generation fighter, the Typhoon is extremely maneuverable in a dogfight and is also able to perform strike missions.

Also representing 41 Squadron is this Typhoon, ZK375. RAF Coningsby is home to 41 Squadron, which is a test and evaluation unit.

An RAF Lockheed C-130J Super Hercules, ZH873, representing 47 Squadron, makes a dusk landing at Nellis AFB. This particular aircraft has since been written off in an accident in 2017.

This RAF C-130, ZH870, is part of 24 Squadron at RAF Brize Norton and is taking off from Nellis AFB to support Red Flag operations.

Fulfilling the aerial refueling mission is the KC3 Voyager, also known as the Airbus A330 MRTT. This Voyager, ZZ337, is from 101 Squadron at RAF Brize Norton.

ABOVE: Another Voyager, ZZ335, has made the trip to Red Flag. The under-wing pods help refuel jets with a probe-and-drogue system.

LEFT: Although primarily an aerial tanker, the Voyager can still transport personnel and cargo inside the main cabin.

To perform electronic surveillance and warfare, the RAF uses the Boeing RC-135W Rivet Joint. This example, ZZ665, is from 51 Squadron, based at RAF Waddington.

To provide battlefield command and control, the Royal Australian Air Force (RAAF) uses the Boeing E-7A Wedgetail, which utilizes a Multi-Role Electronically Scanned Array (MESA) radar mounted on the top of the aircraft.

The Rivet Joint uses sensors all over its airframe to receive communications from a broad spectrum of frequencies. Operators on board interpret and disseminate this information and pass it on to battlefield commanders.

ABOVE: The Wedgetails are based out of RAAF Base Williamtown, and this example, A30-001, is part of No 2 Squadron.

LEFT: The E-7A is based on the Boeing 737-700 airframe and can hold up to 12 crew members depending on its mission.

The RAAF also uses the Boeing EA-18G Growler for electronic attack. The Growler can deny and confuse enemy radar capabilities with its jamming pods.

No 6 Squadron from RAAF Base Amberley operates all 11 of the RAAF's inventory of Growlers.

Australian Growlers use the ALQ-99 jamming pods for electronic warfare and AGM-88 High-speed Anti-Radiation Missiles (HARM) for kinetic options against radars.

The Australian Super Hornet uses the AN/ASQ-228 ATFLIR targeting pod, seen below the port air intake. The ATFLIR helps guide precision munitions, including laser-guided bombs, to their targets in adverse weather conditions.

For strike and air-to-air capabilities, the RAAF employs 24 Boeing F/A-18F Super Hornets. The Super Hornets will be replaced by incoming F-35A Lightning IIs. This Super Hornet, photographed landing, is A44-205.

An excellent example of tail art is shown on this Super Hornet, serial number A44-210, celebrating the centennial anniversary of No 1 Squadron, based at RAAF Amberley.

Super Hornet A44-210 flies overhead on landing approach and shows off its external stores and hard point pylons.

The Aeronatica Militare (Italian Air Force) is represented by their Lockheed Martin F-35A Lightning IIs, and this example, MM7336, arrives at Red Flag and gives a great view of its belly.

Italian Lighting II MM7336 is from 13° Gruppo (13th Group) at Amendola Air Base. The Lighting IIs were activated in 2016.

LEFT: Another Aeronatica Militare participant is the Eurofighter EF-2000 Typhoon. This example, MM7310 36-32, blasts off from Nellis AFB and is from 36° Stormo (36th Wing) at Gioia del Colle Air Base.

BELOW: A perennial participant at Red Flag is the Royal Canadian Air Force (RCAF), which has sent their CC-177 Globemaster III, serial number 177704, representing 429 Transport Squadron at CFB Trenton.

One of the older fighters at Red Flag is the Luftwaffe's (German Air Force) Panavia Tornado IDS, a multi-role strike aircraft. This Tornado, 44+58, is from Taktisches Luftwaffengeschwader 33 (Tactical Air Force Wing 33) at Büchel Air Base.

This Tornado, 44+33, makes its final approach on landing at Nellis AFB. Shown under the starboard centerline pylon is the AN/AAQ(V) Litening Pod, used to provide targeting information for standoff weapons.

Tornados 45+88 and 44+70 fly in formation after taking off from Nellis AFB. They are on their way to an interdiction mission at the Nevada Test and Training Range.

The Luftwaffe Tornados are slated to be replaced in 2025 by a combination of Super Hornets, Growlers, and Typhoons.

This magnificent shot shows two Tornados coming in for a landing. They are banking at steep angles for a quick landing approach.

Eurofighter is comprised of three aerospace companies, including BAE Systems, Airbus, and Leonardo and is a joint venture between Germany, the United Kingdom, Spain, and Italy.

This three-ship formation of Typhoons gets ready for a mission as it passes over Nellis AFB.

Although Red Flag is the largest air combat exercise in the world, other exercises are held throughout NATO, including the famous Tiger Meet, where units, who are named for the big cat, are invited to participate in training. The highlight of the Tiger Meet is the liveries that are painted on the jets. This Ejército del Aire (Spanish Air Force) Typhoon C.16, 14-31, still sports its 2018 Tiger Meet colors on its tail and canards. It is from Ala 14 (Wing 14) at Albacete Air Base.

ABOVE: As this Ejército del Aire Typhoon flies over, two dummy GBU-16 Paveway II laser-guided bombs are visible on the pylons on either side of the air intake.

RIGHT: A magnificent four-ship formation of Ejército del Aire Typhoons heads out on a Red Flag mission as part of the Blue Force.